SCOTLAND'S NEW WRITING THEATRE

Traverse Theatre Company

I was a Beautiful Day

by Iain F MacLeod

cast in order of appearance

Dan	Iain Macrae
Lube	John Kazek
Anne	Lesley Hart

Director	Philip Howard
Designer	Mary Robson
Lighting Designer	Kai Fischer
Composer	Paul Mounsey
Voice Director	Ros Steen
Assistant Director	Annie George
Stage Manager	Lee Davis
Deputy Stage Manager	Gemma Smith
Assistant Stage Managers	Sunita Hinduja/Claire Ramsay
Wardrobe Supervisor	Aileen Sherry

First performed at An Lanntair, Stornoway, Isle of Lewis, on Friday 7 October 2005

TRAVERSE THEATRE

Powerhouse of new writing DAILY TELEGRAPH

Artistic Director Philip Howard

The Traverse is Scotland's new writing theatre. Founded in 1963 by a group of maverick artists and enthusiasts, it began as an imaginative attempt to capture the spirit of adventure and experimentation of the Edinburgh Festival all year round. Throughout the decades, the Traverse has evolved and grown in artistic output and ambition. It has refined its mission by strengthening its commitment to producing new plays by Scottish and international playwrights and actively nurturing them throughout their careers. Traverse productions have been seen worldwide and tour regularly throughout the UK and overseas.

The Traverse has produced over 600 new plays in its lifetime and, through a spirit of innovation and risk-taking, has launched the careers of many of the country's best known writers. From, among others, Stanley Eveling in the 1960s, John Byrne in the 1970s, Liz Lochhead in the 1980s, to David Greig and David Harrower in the 1990s, the Traverse is unique in Scotland in its dedication to new writing. It fulfils the crucial role of providing the infrastructure, professional support and expertise to ensure the development of a dynamic theatre culture for Scotland.

The Traverse's activities encompass every aspect of playwriting and production, providing and facilitating play-reading panels, script-development workshops, rehearsed readings, public playwriting workshops, writers' groups, discussions and special events. The Traverse's work with young people is of supreme importance and takes the form of encouraging playwriting through its flagship education project *Class Act*, as well as the Traverse Young Writers' Group. In 2004, the Traverse took the Class Act project to Russia and also staged *Articulate*, a pilot project with West Dunbartonshire Council for 11 to 14 year olds.

Edinburgh's Traverse Theatre is a mini-festival in itself THE TIMES

From its conception in the 1960s, the Traverse has remained a pivotal venue during the Edinburgh Festival. It receives enormous critical and audience acclaim for its programming, as well as regularly winning awards. In 2002 the Traverse produced award-winning shows, *Outlying Islands* by David Greig and *Iron* by Rona Munro and in 2003, *The People Next Door* by Henry Adam picked up Fringe First and Herald Angel Awards before transferring to the Theatre Royal, Stratford East. Re-cast and with a new director, *The People Next Door* has since toured to Germany, the Balkans and New York. In 2004, the Traverse produced the award-winning *Shimmer* by Linda McLean and a stage adaptation of Raja Shehadeh's diary account of the Israeli occupation of Ramallah, *When The Bulbul Stopped Singing*. This play won the Amnesty International Freedom of Expression Award 2004, appeared in January 2005 as part of the Fadjr International Theatre Festival in Tehran and toured to New York in Spring 2005. The Traverse's Festival 2005 programme received a total of twelve awards, including a Fringe First for its own production, *East Coast Chicken Supper*.

To find out about ways to support the Traverse, please contact Norman MacLeod, Development Manager on 0131 228 3223.

www.traverse.co.uk

Thirteen Years of the Traverse Theatre's Highland Tour & Writers Project

LOOSE ENDS by Stuart Hepburn
GRACE IN AMERICA by Antoine Ò Flatharta
KNIVES IN HENS by David Harrower
FAITH HEALER by Brian Friel
LAZYBED by Iain Crichton Smith
HERITAGE by Nicola McCartney
HIGHLAND SHORTS
seven short plays by Highland & Island writers
AMONG UNBROKEN HEARTS by Henry Adam
THE BALLAD OF CRAZY PAOLA by Arne Sierens
in a version by Stephen Greenhorn
HOMERS by Iain F MacLeod
OUTLYING ISLANDS by David Greig
THE NEST by Alan Wilkins
I WAS A BEAUTIFUL DAY by Iain F MacLeod

I was a Beautiful Day by Iain F MacLeod was commissioned by the Traverse to open the new An Lanntair Arts Centre in Stornoway, Isle of Lewis, before embarking on a tour throughout the Highlands and Islands. This is the first time the Traverse has opened a production outside of its own venue since 1997 (when *Lazybed* opened at The Lemon Tree, Aberdeen) and marks our continued commitment to the annual Highland Tour & Writers Project.

anLanntair

In January 2002, An Lanntair was awarded funds from the Scottish Arts Council National Lottery, Highlands & Islands Special Transitional Programme (ERDF), Western Isles Enterprise and Comhairle nan Eilean Siar (Western Isles Council) to develop a new arts centre on a prime site on the sea front in Stornoway. Designed by architects Nicoll Russell Studios, the development is of key strategic regional importance to the arts and culture in the North West Highlands and is the largest arts development in the Highlands & Islands since Eden Court opened in Inverness in the 1970s.

With thanks to the Scottish Arts Council and Hi-Arts for their consistent support and to Iain F MacLeod and all the playwrights who have, in its thirteen-year history, contributed to the Highland Tour and Writers Project.

Traverse Theatre, September 2005

FOREWORD

I remember a walk I took with my uncle around the curve of cliffs at the north of Ness, the village I come from. The very north of it is called Rubha Robhanis, a word mix of Gaelic and Norse, both words meaning the same thing – headland.

We got out of the car at the lighthouse, noticing a bus-load of people milling around the lighthouse base. We tagged along and smiling knowingly we made it up to the top of the lighthouse. And there it was, the village lying flat like a map beneath us. I remember it now quite calmly, perhaps because the memory of plastering myself like a whelk against the lighthouse glass has faded. Indeed it was a little blowy that day, and the lighthouse is perched on a high cliff, which is gradually disintegrating into the sea.

We carried on with our walk, up past the memory cross where a man once 'went with the cliff' as they say. Each year the cross has to be moved further inland. At various times when I was young, I would remember the Coastguard helicopter appearing and scanning the sea-cliffs. The sea would stream out in strange currents from the beaches, sometimes taking people unawares.

We then came to Luchraban, which they call 'Pygmy Isle'. Small people used to live there, I had once been told. I have looked at the person who told me that strangely ever since.

The tide was out, so it was possible to cross over. My uncle hopped down, although I couldn't see it, couldn't see a way over to the little tidal island. But with much clutching at sea-pink and a final rush over the top I made it onto the small green, pink sward. Two monk's cells and a chapel were buried in the top. It was unexpected to say the least, you could barely make them out from the 'mainland', but here they were, beautiful stonework and snug as anything. I wondered what on earth these people did, hanging off this cliff. Peregrine monks on their little sea island, taking inspiration from the Middle East ascetics. Hiding from Vikings and eating mushrooms. Must have been cold, I thought.

A little further up the coast we clambered down to a massive natural arch called Toll a' Ròidh where the Vikings reputedly tried to pull the island back to Scandinavia. I used to quite like the idea that the Vikings liked the place so much, they wanted to take it home with them. But they didn't manage, of course. The thought that a seafaring people like the Vikings would be so daft was put to the back of our minds.

From there we looked out over Traigh Shanndaidh. This was the beach Saint Ronan left from, on the back of a sea monster, to find his own little monkish spot in the world. This story I particularly liked. Ronan established a church on the edge of the village, but he found the people of the place rather wicked. How so? I thought to myself. This was before casinos and happy hours. Still, the holy man found it a trial. He particularly found it hard to cope with the arguments of the quarrelsome women of the village. So he prayed to be delivered from the place, stipulating that he didn't care where he ended up. Just get me away from these bloody women, he quite possibly added to that night's particular prayer. Stupidly, it turns out.

He was picked up on Traigh Shanndaidh by a 'cianarain-cnò' ('Seven great whales, feast for a cianarain-cnò'), and transported across the waves to the island of Ronaidh, about forty miles north. There, his monkish presence disturbed the beasts that had probably very happily been dwelling there. Nonetheless, they were evil little blighters and were thus forced into the sea, leaving nothing but their scratch marks behind them. And so, after much to-ing and fro-ing, Ronan had the place to himself. As estate agents would say, he most certainly had a 'northerly aspect'. Ronan was later joined by his sister, only to leave sharpish on her brother commenting on what a nice pair of pins she had.

As well as the crazy Vikings and the miniature rock-dwelling monks, I was very fond of Saint Ronan. He seemed to me a passionate fellow. Maybe a little . . . hasty . . . but nonetheless, he didn't stand for any nonsense. It would be unfair to compare the men of the area now to Ronan, but there are some similarities, not least in their escaping to the Social Club to put some space between themselves and the wickedly quarrelsome women of the parish.

I don't know when I started hearing these stories first. Maybe they were just in the air. One thing it did was realign how you thought about the place, the sheer traffic of the area, the fact that you weren't, in fact, remote. It was a veritable motorway! The Vikings landed on this beach! Monks on the run! And here were their stories set in the stone of the land, and set in the language of the people. A place-name for each to remind us. Toll a' Ròidh. Luchraban. Traigh Shanndaidh.

My knowledge of place names is of course terribly eroded. Place names require people to remember them. And for this they need relevance, a relevance which activities such as work provide. That's why the moorland that stretches outwards from the back of the village is littered with place names. By a stroke of luck, I once sat down with a man called Eve from the village who remembered all of them. He reeled them off, but I did wish that I could have walked along the coast with him to learn them properly.

The people of the area didn't rely on maps to find their way. They relied on these place names, which created a frame of reference for them. A kind of virtual village, the interconnected pathways of place names was their GPS to tell them where they were. It hinted at the relationship between words and the places they signify. Embedded in these names were stories. Historical-story DNA buried yet retrievable. This way of looking at the world around you, this prose map, is entirely different to the technical map. When you take into account the stories behind the place names, it can make a normal map look a little bare.

My first cousin in New Zealand, also called Iain, revealed to me that he loved maps. He would sit in his shed and trace imaginary journeys on these maps. When I met him last he had bought a computer programme which let him fly over the topography in any direction he wanted. This delighted him more than any number of pancakes. My uncle has a great collection of maps and has written a book on the mapping of the Western Isles. So maybe there is a rogue cartographic gene in the family. Or maybe, living on an island, one is aware of where the edge is.

I don't want to give the impression that the place is inward-looking, even though it is well detailed and mapped. The other stories I am left with from my youth (other than what happened in the village) are of places such as Buenos Aires, Montreal and New Zealand. A large number of the men of a certain age in the village were in the Merchant Navy. A couple of islanders sailed with Shackleton. One fellow mistakenly asked for a lift home in Sydney Harbour and spent two years eating penguins in Antarctica – it was the ship *Discovery* he asked for a lift.

I once got the chance to film a documentary in the Polynesian Island of Tonga. Filming a girl who was going with the group, I prepared to explain it all to an older fellow sitting in front of the fire, just so he would have an idea of the great distances his girl was going! So he would have an idea where on earth this Tonga was! Before I managed to lay it out for him, however, he took his pipe out of his mouth and said, 'Yes, Tonga. A nice place. I was there three times. Delivering copra.' I learnt that day that a pipe and slippers meant nothing. I have had untold experiences like this. A woman's blank stare after being told that three men in the room (my two uncles and father) had all been to her home island of Pitcairn (of *Mutiny on the Bounty* fame).

One of my uncles ended up in New Zealand. He was on a ship in the Panama Canal on the way home, when he got to talking to another man from Ness on an outward passage. The man's father had died and so they agreed to swap passages. And so, my uncle headed back out to New Zealand, where he met a woman and settled down, but would occasionally walk the harbour and shout out to the ships, 'Any Lewismen on board!'

But talking to him, even after so many years away from Ness, he still remembers the place minutely. He remembers the houses, he remembers people, he can wander at will from place to place, as if he has never spent a moment away from it. And so people carry on remembering the old stories and creating new ones. All in all, it is rather a privilege to be from there, and very handy for someone who from time to time writes a story. Yes indeed.

Iain F MacLeod, September 2005

COMPANY BIOGRAPHIES

Kai Fischer (Lighting Designer) Trained in Audio-Visual Media at the HDM in Stuttgart. For the Traverse: ONE DAY ALL THIS WILL COME TO NOTHING. Other lighting designs for Scottish theatre companies include: ENDGAME, THE DANCE OF DEATH (Citizens'); BEGIN AGAIN, NEXT TIME AROUND (KtC); THE DANNY CROWE SHOW, MERLIN (Dundee Rep); EXPLODING CHESTNUTS ... (Glasgow Nürnberg Dance Alliance); WOYZECK, BLOOD AND ICE (Royal Lyceum, Edinburgh); MARCHING ON (7:84); SWITCHBACK (SweetScar); STROMA (TAG); MACBETH, A DOLL'S HOUSE, THEBANS, UNCLE VANYA, MEDEA, GREEKS (Theatre Babel); BEAUTY AND THE BEAST (Tron/Theatre Babel) and INTO THE DARK (Visible Fictions). Set and lighting designs include: MANCUB, LOST ONES, SAUCHIEHALL STREET, STARS BENEATH THE SEA, INVISIBLE MAN, A BRIEF HISTORY OF TIME, GLIMPSE, LAST STAND (Vanishing Point). Work as Assistant Lighting Designer includes Scottish Opera's recent productions of DAS RHEINGOLD and DIE WALKÜRE with Wolfgang Göbbel, LOHENGRIN (Göteborgs Operan), DIE ZAUBERFLÖTE (Kammeroper Wien), JULIETTA (Opera North), UN BALLO IN MASCHERA (De Vlaamse Opera, Gent) and COSI FAN TUTTE with Zerlina Hughes (Scottish Opera).

Annie George (Assistant Director) Theatre credits as an actor include: DOING BIRD, WITCH DOCTOR, DAYLIGHT ROBBERY (CAT. A. Theatre Company). Radio credits as an actor include: DR FINLAY'S CASEBOOK (BBC Radio 4). Short Film credits include: DADDY'S GIRL (Prix De Jury, Cannes Film Festival and Best Short Film Awards in Paris, Naples, Romania and Avanca Portugal). Credits as a co-producer include: MY DAUGHTER'S FACE (winner of Special Jury Prize, Palm Springs International Short Film Festival). Directing credits include: CURRY AND IRN-BRU (winner of Best Community Film, Real to Reel Glasgow International Film Festival and Satyajit Ray Foundation Award Nomination).

Lesley Hart (*Anne*) Trained: RSAMD. For the Traverse: SHIMMER, OUTLYING ISLANDS, AMONG UNBROKEN HEARTS, SHETLAND SAGA. Other theatre includes: NIGHTINGALE AND CHASE, THE TWITS, A MIDSUMMER NIGHT'S DREAM (Citizens' Theatre); THE DANNY CROWE SHOW (Dundee Rep); TINY DYNAMITE (Paines Plough/Frantic Assembly/Lyric Hammersmith); RUNNING GIRL (Boilerhouse). Television work includes: CASUALTY, PANORAMA – INVISIBLE KIDS (BBC). Radio includes: THE INNOCENCE OF RADIUM, FIFTEEN MINUTES THAT CHANGED THE WORLD, WHOEVER YOU CHOOSE TO LOVE, THE GOLDEN SLIPPER, THE STRANGER AT

THE PALAZZO D'ORO (BBC Radio 4); HIMMLER'S BOY, LYNTON BAY (BBC Radio Scotland); GHOST ZONE (BBC Radio 7).

Philip Howard (Director) Trained under Max Stafford-Clark at the Royal Court Theatre, London, on the Regional Theatre Young Director Scheme from 1988-90. Associate Director at the Traverse from 1993-6, and Artistic Director since 1996. Productions at the Traverse include 17 world premieres of plays by David Greig, David Harrower, Catherine Czerkawska, Catherine Grosvenor, Ronan O'Donnell, Nicola McCartney, Linda McLean, Sue Glover, Iain Heggie, Iain F MacLeod and the late Iain Crichton Smith. Fringe First awards for KILL THE OLD TORTURE THEIR YOUNG, WIPING MY MOTHER'S ARSE and OUTLYING ISLANDS. Other productions at the Traverse include FAITH HEALER by Brian Friel, THE TRESTLE AT POPE LICK CREEK by Naomi Wallace, CUTTIN' A RUG by John Byrne, WHEN THE BULBUL STOPPED SINGING by Raja Shehadeh (also Fadjr International Festival, Tehran; Off-Broadway, New York) and, as Co-Director, SOLEMN MASS FOR A FULL MOON IN SUMMER by Michel Tremblay (also Barbican Centre, London). Productions elsewhere include WORDS OF ADVICE FOR YOUNG PEOPLE by Ioanna Anderson (Rough Magic, Dublin), THE SPECULATOR by David Greig in Catalan (Grec Festival, Barcelona), ENTERTAINING MR SLOANE (Royal, Northampton) and SOMETHING ABOUT US (Lyric Hammersmith Studio). Radio: BEING NORWEGIAN by David Greig (BBC Scotland).

John Kazek (*Lube*) Trained: RSAMD. For the Traverse: THE SLAB BOYS TRILOGY, SOLEMN MASS FOR A FULL MOON IN SUMMER (Traverse/Barbican), KING OF THE FIELDS, PERFECT DAYS (Traverse/ Vaudeville), PASSING PLACES, CHIC NERDS, STONES AND ASHES, EUROPE. Other theatre includes: KNIVES IN HENS (TAG); HEDDA GABLER, MACBETH, THEBANS, UNCLE VANYA, 'TIS PITY SHE'S A WHORE (Theatre Babel); WORD FOR WORD (Magnetic North); PLEASURE AND PAIN, GLUE, A MIDSUMMER NIGHT'S DREAM (Citizens' Theatre); MARABOU STORK NIGHTMARE (Citizens'/ Leicester); VARIETY (Grid Iron); THE BIG FUNK (Arches); PENETRATOR (Tron); MARY QUEEN OF SCOTS, KIDNAPPED (Lyceum); TWILIGHT SHIFT (7:84/Edinburgh Festival); WUTHERING HEIGHTS, DRIVING MISS DAISY (Byre), KING LEAR, AS YOU LIKE IT (Oxford Stage Company). Television work includes: THE KEY (BBC/Little Bird); AUF WIEDERSEHEN PET, CITY CENTRAL, DOUBLE NOUGAT, RAB C NESBITT, PUNCH DRUNK, STRATHBLAIR (BBC); TAGGART, HIGH ROAD (STV). Film includes: BATMAN BEGINS (Warner Bros); DEAR FRANKIE (Scorpio Films); HOW D'YAE WANT TAE DIE (Dead Man's Shoes Ltd); YOUNG ADAM (Film Council/Hanway Films); RIFF RAFF (Parallax Pictures); SILENT SCREAM (Antonine Productions)

Iain F MacLeod (Writer) For the Traverse: HOMERS, ALEXANDER SALAMANDER, ROAD FROM THE ISLES and MISTER SEQUESTER (Un Homme en Faillite), which was performed as a rehearsed reading. Other theatre credits include: MAIRI ANNDRA'S HOUSE (A musical for children); SALVAGE (Tosg Theatre Company); CLIFF DANCING (National Gaelic Youth Theatre). His writing for TV/Radio includes: THE WATERGAW (RADIO 4), MACHAIR (STV), COLOURS (EOLAS FOR BBC). Novels include THE KLONDYKERS and a novel for teenagers called CHOPPER. TV and Film directing experience includes: A documentary for the BBC about nva's performance THE STORR: UNFOLDING LANDSCAPE (Zebo Productions); MURDO MACFARLANE – THE MELBOST BARD (Best Arts Documentary, Celtic Film and TV Festival 2001), TACSI (BBC SCOTLAND, BAFTA Award for Best Arts Programme, Best Entertainment Programme, Celtic Film and TV Festival). Iain is Writer in Residence at Sabhal Mòr Ostaig in Skye, and also plays guitar with The Anna Murray Band.

Iain Macrae (Dan) Trained: Mountview Theatre School, London. For the Traverse: SHIMMER, HOMERS, HERITAGE, HIGHLAND SHORTS, THE TRESTLE AT POPE LICK CREEK, LAZYBED, PASSING PLACES. Other theatre includes: MARY, QUEEN OF SCOTS GOT HER HEAD CHOPPED OFF (Prime Productions); JEKYLL & HYDE (Mull Theatre); BEGIN AGAIN (KTC Theatre Company); HOUSES OF THE SEA (Tosg Theatre); PHAEDRA'S LOVE (Ghostown/Citizens'); AIPPLE TREE (Dràma na h-Alba); SACRED GROUND (Watford Palace); THE SLAB BOYS (Peacock Theatre); MEMORANDUM, AFTER MAGRITTE (Zone Theatre). Television work includes: CROWDIE AND CREAM, KILLING OF THE RED FOX, INTERROGATION OF A HIGHLAND LASS, DWELLY, RAN DAN, YEAR OF THE PRINCE (BBC); THE PLAN MAN (Channel 4); MACHAIR, AIPPLE TREE, ICE CREAM MACHINE (STV). Voice for numerous TV cartoons, and extensive work for radio. Film includes: THE GIFT, MAIRI MHOR (BBC); AS AN EILEAN (C4). Short films include: BEFORE WINTER WINDS, COLOURS (BBC). Iain has recently completed a drama documentary on Neil Munro and the comedy series COMADAIDH OIR, both to be broadcast by the BBC.

Paul Mounsey (Composer) Trained: Trinity College of Music, London. Paul is a Scottish composer who lived for many years in Brazil, where he enjoyed considerable success composing for television, film, advertising and also for the Latin American pop market. His work has ranged from the Brazilian mini-series CITY OF MEN to the music for VisitScotland's ad campaign to music for nva's THE STORR: UNFOLDING LANDSCAPE event. Music from his solo albums has been consistently used on UK and US television. He's written pop hits for Mexican boy bands, had chamber works performed on BBC Radio 3, and he has lived with and recorded the music of indigenous communities in the Amazon rainforest. He currently lives on the Isle of Skye.

Mary Robson (Designer) Trained: Wimbledon School of Art. For the Traverse: LOOSE ENDS, GRACE IN AMERICA, HOMERS. Other theatre includes: WISE GUYS (Red Ladder and Contact Theatre). Opera includes costume design for PUNCH AND JUDY (Aldeburgh Festival and tour). Arts in Health work includes: COMMON KNOWLEDGE, HAPPY HEARTS, ROOTS AND WINGS (Project Director), CAHHM (Centre for Arts and Humanities in Health and Medicine, University of Durham- Research Associate). Mary has recently been awarded a three year NESTA Fellowship to commence in November 2005, allowing her to build on practice as an artist and social educator, working closely with communities.

Ros Steen (Voice Director) Trained: RSAMD. Has worked extensively in theatre, film and TV. For the Traverse: EAST COAST CHICKEN SUPPER, IN THE BAG, THE SLAB BOYS TRILOGY, DARK EARTH, HOMERS, OUTLYING ISLANDS, THE BALLAD OF CRAZY PAOLA, THE TRESTLE AT POPE LICK CREEK, HERITAGE (2001 and 1998), AMONG UNBROKEN HEARTS, SHETLAND SAGA, SOLEMN MASS FOR A FULL MOON IN SUMMER (as co-director), KING OF THE FIELDS, HIGHLAND SHORTS, FAMILY, KILL THE OLD TORTURE THEIR YOUNG, CHIC NERDS, GRETA, LAZYBED, KNIVES IN HENS, PASSING PLACES, BONDAGERS, ROAD TO NIRVANA, SHARP SHORTS, MARISOL, GRACE IN AMERICA. Other theatre credits include: MYSTERY OF THE ROSE BOUQUET, A HANDFUL OF DUST, CLEO, CAMPING, EMANUELLE AND DICK; A WHISTLE IN THE DARK, A LITTLE BIT OF RUFF (Citizens' Theatre); THE GRADUATE, A LIE OF THE MIND, MACBETH, TWELFTH NIGHT, DANCING AT LUGHNASA (Dundee Rep); THE WONDERFUL WORLD OF DISSOCIA (EIF/Drum Theatre, Plymouth/Tron); UNCLE VARICK, PLAYBOY OF THE WESTERN WORLD (Royal Lyceum, Edinburgh); THE SMALL THINGS (Paines Plough); MANCUB (Vanishing Point). Film credits include: GREYFRIARS BOBBY (Piccadilly Pictures); GREGORY'S TWO GIRLS (Channel Four Films). Television credits include: SEA OF SOULS, 2000 ACRES OF SKY, MONARCH OF THE GLEN, HAMISH MACBETH (BBC).

SPONSORSHIP

Sponsorship income enables the Traverse to commission and produce new plays and to offer audiences a diverse and exciting programme of events throughout the year. We would like to thank the following companies for their support:

CORPORATE SPONSORS

B B C Scotland

T H E **H A L L I O N**

Canon

NICHOLAS
GROVES
RAINES
ARCHITECTS

ANNIVERSARY ANGELS

With thanks to

Claire Aitken of Royal Bank of Scotland for mentoring support
arranged through the Arts & Business Mentoring Scheme.
Purchase of the Traverse Box Office, computer network and
technical and training equipment has been made possible with
money from The Scottish Arts Council National Lottery Fund

The Traverse Theatre's work
would not be possible without the support of

The Traverse Theatre receives financial assistance from

The Calouste Gulbenkian Foundation, The Peggy Ramsay Foundation, The Binks Trust, The Bulldog Prinsep Theatrical Fund, The Esmée Fairbairn Foundation, The Gordon Fraser Charitable Trust, The Garfield Weston Foundation, The Paul Hamlyn Foundation, The Craignish Trust, Lindsay's Charitable Trust, The Tay Charitable Trust, The Ernest Cook Trust, The Wellcome Trust, The Sir John Fisher Foundation, The Ruben and Elisabeth Rausing Trust, The Equity Trust Fund, The Cross Trust, N Smith Charitable Settlement, Douglas Heath Eves Charitable Trust, The Bill and Margaret Nicol Charitable Trust, The Emile Littler Foundation, Mrs M Guido's Charitable Trust, Gouvernement du Québec, The Canadian High Commission, The British Council, The Daiwa Foundation, The Sasakawa Foundation, The Japan Foundation

Charity No. SC002368

Sets, props and costumes for
I WAS A BEAUTIFUL DAY
created by Traverse Workshops
(funded by the National Lottery)

Scottish
Arts Council
LOTTERY FUNDED

Production photography by Douglas Robertson
Print photography by Euan Myles

For their continued generous support
of Traverse productions the Traverse thanks

Habitat, Marks and Spencer, Princes Street
Camerabase, BHS, and Holmes Place

For their help on I WAS A BEAUTIFUL DAY,
the Traverse thanks

Kelly Davidson

For their support, inspiration and occasional lodgings
Iain Finlay MacLeod would like to thank:

Philip Howard and Mary Robson. Susie Mathews, Peter May and Janice in France, Philip Gibb and Julie Baikie in Australia, Hannah Rye. David 'Doctor Kildare' Sheasby. Alex MacDonald and everyone at An Lanntair. All the staff at the Traverse. And Sabhal Mòr Ostaig for letting me be their writer-in-residence.

TRAVERSE THEATRE – THE COMPANY

I WAS A BEAUTIFUL DAY

Iain F MacLeod

Dha Fionnlagh

Characters

DAN MORRISON, *male, fifty years of age. He is a patient at Dunard. From the village of Robhanis*

LUBE, *male, mid-thirties to forties. He is a patient at Dunard. He is from Glasgow*

ANNE WILLIAMS, *female, mid-thirties. Works for Ordnance Survey*

A dash (–) indicates that a character is interrupted.

A forward slash (/) indicates that the next character starts speaking at that point.

This text went to press before the end of rehearsals so may differ slightly from the play as performed.

ACT ONE

A room in Dunard Psychiatric Unit, 2005. It is an old Victorian-style building on mainland Scotland.

DAN *is in the room. He carefully repositions a chair which has gone awry. Makes sure the bed is exact. He starts to write.*

DAN.
A landmark.
A seamark.
A traverse between two points.
A comharr.
A comharr is something which tethers you
Marks your place
Between land and sea
Only marked by the jagged snaim of cliffs
Or white comb of wave
Bird's eye only sees it but
There it is.
It moves into position
A green sward with a tulach of rock
Cairn-tipped green with your
Gneiss-lined longtitude
A straight tether
Bacan
This is what I need
Some kind of feist rope straight
As a finger pointed
To tie me to earth
That invisible line
Which says to me
You are here
You have arrived
You know your purpose.
We all need this. We all need a comharr. Places named. Anchors.
Leac Ard. Rubha Sgeir. Meall Dubh. An Carbh . . .

LUBE, *another patient, pokes his head around the door.*

LUBE. Konichiwa mein freunde, I was just passing and . . .

DAN *goes over to the door and shuts it in* LUBE's *face. A moment passes and then a little knock at the door. It gently eases open again.*

I was just passing and . . .

DAN s*huts the door in* LUBE's *face again. It slowly creaks open again.*

I was just . . .

DAN. Will you please stop.

Pause.

LUBE. I was just passing and I noticed that your door was ajar. And . . . anyway, I was just passing and saw you scribbling away like a chicken that's won the lottery.

DAN. This is my room. I'm doing something.

DAN *starts to tidy up his papers.*

LUBE. That's what I'm saying. Gog-gag. What it could be I haven't an earthly . . .

DAN. This is private property. Please leave me alone. Sneaking up on me. You make a habit of sneaking up on unsuspecting people at their business? Please go.

LUBE. Only if you'll tell me what you're up to.

DAN. Writing. I can write in my own room if I want to.

Pause. LUBE *still stands in the door. He looks at four stones that are on the floor. He picks one up.*

LUBE. Building a very small wall?

DAN. You're still standing there . . .

LUBE. . . . enjoying my new-found freedom.

DAN. Freedom. New-found?

LUBE. Yes! Today is a happy day. For exactly that reason. Can I come in? We can share a celebratory. A suspicion of whisky if we had any. But a moment will do.

DAN. I'm not sure. I'm not happy with this inveigling. Something I'm not entirely enamelled with.

LUBE. I'm celebrating because I've been downgraded.

DAN. That doesn't sound so good.

LUBE *tries to step into the room.*

Back! Step back.

4

LUBE. I sense you have issues with visitors.

DAN. I just like things . . .

LUBE. Very well, very good. Now. Like I was saying, I've been downgraded. Or is it upgraded? One sometimes doesn't know if one's grade is going up or down these days. Anyway! That's why they've sent me here. This is much more unflusterable and pleasant-making. That's why I have the air somewhat of the Buddhist monk about me. No trouble. See.

A pause while LUBE *is no trouble.*

I'm not a problem, you see.

DAN. Well. That's good.

LUBE. You seem quietly disapproving.

DAN. No, it's just . . .

LUBE. Must be hard for one so prickly to make friends.

DAN. You hardly know me!

LUBE *steps fully into the room.*

LUBE. Oh well, I'll be glad to make your acquaintance properly, thanks very much for inviting me in. Let me introduce myself . . .

DAN. Get out! Get out, get out, get out!

LUBE. What's wrong with you!

DAN. I'll have you reminded that this is my room!

LUBE. Come now. We're all in this together. What what?

DAN. What part of 'I said get out' didn't you understand! Yet your mouth keeps spraching forth words like a thrush.

LUBE. Did you know thrushes can imitate other animals?

Pause.

DAN. What?

LUBE. And cats can impersonate birds!

DAN. I'm going to have to ask you to leave. This really is the biggest load of nonsense I've ever set eyes on.

LUBE. I've heard it happen! Cats! Birds! No . . . listen. No . . . listen. And then they swallow them. One minute friend. The next, you're being eating by this whiskered beast! Meowing with delight as it licks the marrow from your little legs! What

kind of world is this we live in if cats can pretend to be birds
and thrushes can pretend to be diggers? You heard me. Diggers.
I've heard it. Me! Yes! Yours truly!

DAN grabs him and yanks him fully into the room.

DAN. A mouth like the mouth of the day! You'll attract all sorts of
attention to us with your carrying on and your mouth without a
button.

Pause.

LUBE. I'll be as quiet as the proverbial grave.

LUBE *goes over to the door. He opens it. He shuts it. He opens
it. He shuts it.*

DAN. Please stop that.

LUBE. A-OK. First class. Happy, happy. I sometimes forget I'm free
to roam like a buffalo at home . . . what is that song? On the plains
when they . . . dum-de-dum . . . sing a bit all day. No. Anyway,
best keep a low profile for me just now. The security officers
here are as prickly as gurnards. Like gurnards the whole lot of
them with their spiky keys. Personally, I like the doctors better.

Pause.

But I couldn't eat a whole one.

Pause.

What are you doing here, anyway?

DAN. I thought we'd established this was my room.

LUBE. No no no. Case history, I mean.

DAN. I'd rather not speak about it. That's very forward.

LUBE. What difference does it make?

Pause.

DAN. I get pains. In the head. Rashes. Tiredness. Like little
sweeties in a bottle all bubbling around inside me. Things come
back to me.

LUBE. Like kippers.

DAN. What?

LUBE. Kippers come back on me something awful.

DAN. No. I see things. They happen as if they're happening for
the first time. It is not kippers I am talking about. You're
obviously not taking it seriously.

6

LUBE. Pontius Pilate couldn't be more serious. Where from comest these maladies?

DAN. What business is it of yours?

LUBE. Oh, just making breezy chat.

DAN. Are you . . . are you working here? Are you here to check up on me?

LUBE. Of course not.

DAN. I don't trust you.

LUBE. Suit yourself.

Pause.

DAN. The army.

LUBE. An army man! Get a lot of them in here. Most gone with the chaff now.

DAN. They use you. Then when you're broken they throw you away. Like little dolls.

LUBE. Well-armoured dolls, though. Well-trained dolls. Dolls with guns. We'll meet again! Don't know when! Well. That's why you're here, then. Isn't it, obviously! The thick plop of shells all around you. Your head is full of shells. Like a cliff full of winkles. Not above the water long enough to keep the head above water.

Pause.

The Falklands? The Balkans? The Gulf?

DAN. The Gulf. Helping Kuwaitis.

LUBE. So what did you do to end up in here? Something awful, if you're still here after . . . counting counting . . . about fifteen years. You must have gone bananas.

DAN. Look, I was in the middle of something when you barged in.

LUBE. Called by.

DAN. Barged in.

LUBE. Popped my head in.

DAN. Barged in.

LUBE. Said a quick hello.

DAN. There is nothing quick about this hello.

LUBE. A hello is a hello is a hello.

DAN. If you cause trouble I presume they can put you back into your high-security box.

LUBE. Oh, you wouldn't do that. Come on now, joking aside, you wouldn't do that.

DAN. If you carry on barging about . . .

LUBE. No barges. I promise. Come on, joking aside . . .

DAN. Someone . . . might.

LUBE. I'll be like . . . the mouse.

DAN. Good. Glè mhath. ('*Glay va.*')

Pause.

LUBE. Where from?

DAN. I'm from an island. On the west coast of –

LUBE. I know that, don't insult my intelligence. Where from?

DAN. I'm from a village.

LUBE. In the name of the wee man. Will you no start naming names.

DAN. Robhanis.

LUBE. Well, well. Hector himself sprung to life from the Greek soil of the long island. So you speak it, do you, my hero? My warrior. The language of Eden?

DAN. Yes.

LUBE. And here we are. In this shit hole. Speaking English to one another. What a laugh.

DAN. English.

LUBE. Queen's English. Like a fucking English lord's mine is as fresh and clear as the newly raised heads of newborn daffodils.

DAN. That's hardly surprising, is it?

LUBE. Why? How?

DAN. That's what you talk. In Glasgow. Sort of.

LUBE. Yes, I am a personage of Glaswegian orientation. But the blood is undoubtedly of the islands variety. I have an inexplicable longing for the sea, but a constant worry about drowning, even whilst standing at the kitchen table. I like happy songs which end in massacres. I like boiled food. And I have two sets of words careering around inside my head like two sets of rampaging huns donkey-dancing in the clagainn. You know. Strictly speaking. We shouldn't get on.

DAN. We don't.

LUBE. Ah. Ah ha ha.

Pause.

DAN. Speak some Gaelic, then.

LUBE. I don't like to be put upon the spot.

DAN. Say something.

LUBE. I assure you, it would be no trouble for me to.

DAN. I don't believe a word you say. You're a Glaswegian and that's the end of it.

LUBE *goes over to the door. Opens it. Shuts it. Opens it. Shuts it.*

LUBE. Well, it's lucky for you I find you half-entertaining. Or I'd be out of here quicker than a whippet with a ham sandwich.

DAN. It'll be your own company you'll be keeping if you carry on being so rude.

LUBE. Prickly little cratur, aren't we? Mr Anenome. Mr Crubag.

DAN. You said you didn't speak Gaelic.

LUBE. Did I? Well, I do. I used to spend all my summers there at one time. Family from there, so we are. That's where I grew up.

DAN. No it wasn't.

LUBE. I assure you. It was. The beautiful islands. I look back on them now and I can only see them through a haze of nostalgia and summer days and my older cousin with the sun on her skin after her swimming in the cold sea and her T-shirt sticking to her. Those magical words. Abba. I thank the Lord for tight, wet Abba T-shirts. Happy days. Like so many . . . jewels. The islands. Dropped out of a god's pocket. That's what they say. Like diamonds. Like potatoes.

Pause.

Wouldn't you love a potato now?

DAN. It would be nice. I'm not afraid to admit that. A potato of the island variety.

LUBE. The island! Where do you think I spend most of my time? Not in these boxy rooms. Not in this loony-bin, pardon me, no offence. I imagine all the time I imagine you do too I imagine. I imagine I'm by myself. I imagine it with no one there. I don't want to imagine other people. I imagine what it was like when the land was clean and pure. Before the stone-raisers and the holy men and the men from the North. By myself I am. The quiet patient ground waiting for someone. Not one potato planted there! And then the Norsemen arrive with their golden wonders.

DAN. Norsemen.

LUBE. They say it was so beautiful they wanted to take it home with them. Or something like that.

DAN. They looped a rope. Of hair. Is that the story?

LUBE. I couldn't say. I thought you wanted me to go.

DAN. It was women's hair. Maidens. With white skin and long dark armada hair. Around and through the sea cliff-hole and . . . Rowed! Trying they tried to pull the islands they loved back to Scandinavia. The rope strained and popped and . . . but it didn't move. It was tethered by curled gneiss. They pumped and pumped their oars until, like a big snake! Snap! Curl and patterned air and shards of rope everywhere! Our hero. Their captain. Killed. Like a goat.

LUBE. As unceremoniously as that, you say.

DAN. I say. And so they left. And left the island behind them. And that place is called. Toll a' Ròidh . . . Toll a' Ròidh . . .

DAN *goes over to his writing materials and starts to draw something.*

LUBE. There you go again. All this writing, writing, writing . . . What is it?

LUBE *picks up one of the drawings.*

What is this?

DAN *stops.*

DAN. Please put it down.

LUBE. Tell me what it is.

DAN. If you put it down I'll tell you something. I wasn't going to. But I will.

LUBE. Go on.

DAN. I got a visitor today. A visitor previous to your visit. Which I just want to flag up as being not a little unusual.

LUBE. Who was it?

DAN. I don't know.

LUBE. Sounds interesting.

DAN. I . . . I hid.

LUBE. Why?

DAN. I don't know.

LUBE. Maybe it's a soldier thing. Who was it? What did they want?

DAN. To talk to me.

LUBE. Oh yes? Are they coming back?

DAN. The doctor said they would be back at three.

LUBE. They? How many?

DAN. One. Her.

LUBE. Her. Nice.

DAN. I don't know why she wanted to talk to me.

LUBE. Well. That clears it all up, Watson.

Pause.

You can call me Lube.

DAN. Lube. You can call me Dan. That's my name.

Pause.

What's wrong with you, then? I've told you why I'm in here.

LUBE. Nothing that couldn't happen to anybody. The membrane between our lives and total disaster is so thin, even the smallest slip might break it. Don't look down or you might realise that there's actually no one there to catch you if you fall. Wife. Child. House. Armani suits. Slippers. Beach balls. Gone with the wind.

DAN. Your wife?

LUBE. Ex-wife. The bitch! It's because of her I'm in here.

DAN. Is it?

LUBE. Not really. If I was to look at it even-handedly, which I'd rather not do, she did hang in there for a long time. But now . . . she won't even let me see my wee girl. I've got a wee girl.

DAN. Maybe when you get out . . .

LUBE. I had a good job, you know. I was in business. People listened to me. Tell me one thing. Have you ever gone a whole day in here without thinking one thought. Not one?

DAN. No.

LUBE. Hmm. And what language didn't you think that thought in? It's just a question you realise. Just a question.

DAN. The English quite often when I do think. The Gaelic sometimes. But sometimes it's not words. Sometimes I'm just . . . back there.

LUBE. Well, that's interesting, isn't it? I thought I was in an original situation myself and so it's fascinating to meet a cratur of the same leanings. I feel it slipping away. Words. One by one they slip away until . . . maybe one day . . . I won't remember the word for . . . a bed. Leabaidh. Which is bed. Or for a door. Doras. A door. Or for myself. Duine. A man. Mac an duine.

DAN. I feel it.

LUBE *stands near the window.*

LUBE. Did you feel that?

DAN. What?

LUBE. That breath of wind.

DAN. The window's open.

LUBE. Like standing on the cliff edge with the carpet of sea in front of you. Feel that cool salt breeze on. Can you? Salt lips and damp cheeks. Just feel it! The freedom. The hum of the sea rubbing against the rocks. The sound of lobsters. Clickety-clack they go in their little seaweed beds. Oh, all of creation is in my pocket.

DAN. I have no doubt.

LUBE. It's amazing how you can escape. If you just close your eyes tightly for long enough you can escape. Look at me just now, Dan. On the edge of the islands. I stretch my arms and hold the bent circle of the earth in them. The sea scattered with little black pebbles. Tell me another story, Dan.

DAN. Why?

LUBE. Because I like them. They pass the time. Better than being stranded on this . . . this gannety shit-covered rock –

DAN. Like Ronan.

LUBE. Ronan?

DAN. Naomh Ronan. The Saint Ronan. The peregrine. The anchorite.

LUBE. Remind me . . . remind me . . . Come on, Dan. Help me out here.

DAN. God spoke to him. He told him to leave his home. The place was full of heathens.

LUBE. Heathens! That's right! Just like this place, stuffed to the rafters with heathens and sodomites! More! More! You be God.

DAN. Sorry?

LUBE. You be God. Telling me to leave.

DAN. OK. Although I'm not entirely comfortable . . .

LUBE. Come on, Dan!

DAN. OK. (*Voice of God.*) You must leave here. This place is not pure enough any more. Filthy it is. Filthy filthy filthy. How was that?

LUBE. Excellent. Excellent God voice.

DAN. And then a great beast came. Seal-backed and mountain-skinned. And it took him on his back. And he set off from Traigh Shanndaidh, the gold-shelled beach of sorrows. And he was torn from the gut of his island and cast into the desert of the sea, and brought to the island. Ronan's island. Rònaidh. When his foot hit that beautiful soft grass the island shook with the holy man's great padded digits. And the fight with the beasts began.

LUBE. Beasts? Excellent! I like a good fight with beasts. I'll be the beast.

DAN. Who will I be?

LUBE. In the name of the wee man, Dan! You're Saint Ronan!

DAN. Right.

Pause.

LUBE. Well? Banish me!

DAN. He-hem. (*Voice of God.*) I banish thee.

LUBE's *beast is banished under the bed.* .

LUBE. This is really . . . this is really something . . . this is better than two weeks in Tenerife. Better than a woman with small hands rubbing your feet. More, there's more to it . . .

DAN. Brenhilda. His sister.

LUBE. Yes. I remember that bit. Stuck on an island right enough. I'll be Brenhilda . . . right . . . the dirty so-and-so, his own sister, sneaking up to her and stealing little glances until finally he pounced . . .

LUBE makes to kiss DAN.

DAN. Get off me!

LUBE. What . . . what's wrong?

DAN. What are you doing?

LUBE. Telling the story. Acting it out.

DAN. You've spoiled it.

LUBE. But we haven't finished it. He cast her out. Like Eve. Like us.

Pause.

What's wrong?

DAN. Stay over there.

LUBE. What's wrong with you?

DAN. Don't come near me. I'm not that way inclinationed.

LUBE. Fair enough.

They settle down again.

Awfully sorry. Wrong impression and all that.

DAN. It's OK.

Pause.

LUBE. How's this for a plan?

DAN. A plan?

LUBE. A plan. For Dan. Dan's plan.

DAN. Well, strictly speaking, it's your plan.

LUBE. Och! Chopping hairs! Hear me out. With your footery brilliance and handy claws, all we have to do is . . . get the necessary tools to begin . . . yes . . . I reveal it, no . . . yes, no, hold on . . . I present to you . . . the tunnel. Yes. A tunnel out under the wall. Under the perimeter. And then we break out and head south like a herd of geese. Way, way south until the weather is hot. Morocco. Who'll find us there?

DAN. What do we do with the soil from the tunnel?

LUBE. I see. I see how your mind works. Nothing wrong with that. I can be the one with vision and you can put the coal in the boiler. Right then. Here it is. An ingenious system of pulleys in your trousers will deposit it on the golf course.

DAN. It sounds strangely familiar. And rather ill-thought out and impractical.

LUBE. Well, we've got to do something. We've got to get out of here.

DAN. I'm voluntary. I volunteered to come here.

LUBE. What? Why?

DAN. My head was splitting.

LUBE. Come on. We can come up with something together. I think we get on, don't we?

DAN. Well . . .

LUBE. Don't we?

DAN. Sometimes.

LUBE. We've got a connection. Instant. Don't deny it. I don't want to head off by myself into the sunset. I need a compadre. It wasn't . . . Butch Cassidy and . . . his poke of sandwiches. Was it? Compadres. Amigos. Kameraden. And don't think I'd ask anyone else to come with me.

DAN. There must be a reason you're in here. It must be to help you.

LUBE. We can build an aeroplane.

DAN. I don't want to!

LUBE. You'd have been useless in Colditz! Best be careful. Else you'll be left behind.

DAN. How do you mean?

LUBE. You'll wake up one morning and you'll be looking at an old man. And you'll look back on this moment and think, I wish I'd met a man with a plan. And I've got a plan. To get out.

DAN. I'm just . . . I know where things are here. I . . . I don't know if it's able for me.

LUBE. Come on, Dan. A beach. The sun hot on your back. The blue horizon. A cold beer in your paw. Freedom.

LUBE *sees a picture beside* DAN*'s bed. He picks it up and looks at it.*

What's this?

DAN. Nothing.

LUBE. Or should I say who is this? Who is this I say?

DAN. A friend. I'd ask you not to go poking around in my room. And I'd ask you to not shift the chairs. I'd ask you to be as still as possible.

LUBE. A friend. A lady friend. Who is the lady? Is that why you won't come? Still hanging on to some dusty fantasy that she'll wait for you? She looks rather nice. A Brenhilda maybe. Maybe you already know her salty tang and what it feels like to be taken in these soft arms.

DAN. Don't say that. Don't say anything about her.

LUBE. Oh? Do I sense a little loving interest? An old flame maybe?

DAN. Give it back.

LUBE. You haven't told me anything yet. Tell me, was she good? Maybe the only one, eh? Behind the cruach stack on a summer's night with the moon low above the horizon and your trousers at your ankles.

DAN runs at him to get the picture back. LUBE *avoids him.*

I have no doubt she's getting it elsewhere now. It's time to move on, Dan. Let it go.

DAN runs at him again and holds him to the ground.

DAN. If you do that again . . . you say things again, I'll kill you.

LUBE. Sorry. Dan . . . sorry.

DAN. I want you to leave.

DAN gets up.

LUBE. Sorry. I'm sorry, Dan. I didn't mean . . . I sometimes forget.

LUBE sits quietly for a while.

Forgive me. I was getting carried away, you see. It's so invigorating not to be yourself for a while.

DAN. I don't know about that.

Pause.

Maybe . . .

There is a knock at the door. LUBE *and* DAN *jump a little.*

16

LUBE. What was that? Who was that?

DAN. I don't know.

LUBE. Jesus Christ! Maybe they heard us . . . it's the . . . it's the . . . hide!

LUBE tries to find a place to hide. The first place he tries is too small. Then LUBE dives under the bed, but it is a bit tight so he only manages to get his torso under, his bum is sticking up into the air.

DAN. Amazing. Like the chameleon himself.

LUBE extricates himself. We hear a woman's voice through the door. It is ANNE.

ANNE. Mr Morrison? Are you in?

LUBE. Quiet now! Ignore this Helen's plaintive wailing, Dan. Ignore it! Don't be a prick-teased Paris.

ANNE. Dan? Yoo-hoo! Are you in there?

DAN. Just coming!

LUBE. What did you say that for?

DAN. She was calling out my name. It's only polite.

LUBE. You must have fallen down the numptie tree and hit each branch on the way down.

DAN. Go on, get out.

LUBE. How exactly?

DAN. Through the window. Come on.

LUBE. No chance. How undignified.

DAN (*to* ANNE). Just coming! (*To* LUBE.) Hide in the corner. Behind the door.

LUBE. What if she comes in with a flourish? She'll break my nose.

DAN. I'll open the door.

LUBE. This is pure Russian roulette, what you're suggesting. Why can't I just make like a normal person past her? A quick hello.

Pause.

DAN. That's a point.

Pause.

LUBE. It'd be embarrassing.

LUBE *stands behind the door. Gives* DAN *the thumbs up. He opens it.*

DAN. Hello.

ANNE. Dan, is it?

DAN. Yes.

ANNE. I'm Anne.

Pause.

Can I come in?

DAN. Um . . . yes . . .

She shakes his hand. Something DAN *isn't used to. He goes over to the window. She follows him.*

I was just looking out of the window.

ANNE. Lovely. It's a nice day for it.

DAN. I quite often like to look out of the window.

ANNE. Is there a nice view?

DAN. Grass. And some trees.

LUBE *sneaks out behind her.* DAN *is momentarily distracted.*

ANNE. Yes, amazing grounds. It's a nice place, isn't it? I was expecting, well, I don't know what I was expecting. It's a big old gothic place. So you expect, you know, bats in the belfry. Jack Nicholson doing the gardening. But you've got a golf course. And a cappuccino machine. That's quite exciting. Shall we grab a coffee? Do you have time to grab a coffee?

DAN. Ehm.

ANNE. Sorry about the 'Yoo-hoo'. I never normally do that. But I liked the way the noise was echoing in the corridor. I don't want to sound mental.

Pause.

DAN. I don't do much . . . yoo-hooing. Myself.

ANNE. Me neither. Just once in a while.

Pause.

DAN. Well. That's lovely to meet you and best of luck.

ANNE. What? I've only just got here. A coffee? They do lattes as well. I presume they do take-out. Maybe they don't.

DAN. I'm fine, thanks.

ANNE. Sorry, I'm talking too much. It's just good to be here at last. It wasn't bad, red-tape-wise. But you know how people in places like this can be sometimes.

DAN. And why are you here?

ANNE. Someone told me that you know more than anybody about the place names of the village you come from.

DAN. You've been there?

ANNE. Yes! I've been working there for a while now. I work for Ordnance Survey. (*She shows him her work pass.*) Between you and me, it's a little boring. Not the work. I love the actual work. It's just living for so long somewhere so remote. I'm living thirty miles from the nearest cappuccino machine.

DAN. I can barely imagine what you're going through.

ANNE. Oh, it's not so bad, I guess. I was working on much more advanced techniques before I was sent up there. Although the theory behind it hasn't changed much for years. And I'm enjoying doing the physical side of it again. On the ground. Wandering around with my theodolite. Although it's not a theodolite, it's all GPS now, but . . . Anyway, we've got the basics from the previous maps. They want me to do another sweep on the place names. They did it in the eighties. But it's hard to find people who know them in detail now. Anyway, tart it up a bit, add some more names and that's me.

DAN. And you want me to . . . do the tarting.

ANNE. Yes. But you don't actually have to bake anything. Get it?

Pause.

There'll be a fee in it for you as well. Not much. But better than nothing, that's what I think, anyway.

DAN. You can keep your money for shoes and caramels.

Pause.

ANNE. I don't want to give you the impression that / this is an awful lot of work.

DAN. This is so tiring.

ANNE. Maybe I've come at a bad time.

DAN. The fact that for some inexplicable reason my room has turned into Bartholomew Fair today is not the only botheration. No. You come in here wanting, no . . . expecting, me to give you everything you want without even a packet of biscuits in tow –

ANNE. I thought we could go to the café.

DAN. – and then you proceed to talk about how much you dislike staying up there, can't wait to get away so you can buy lots of things and fill your face with pastries –

ANNE. What does that mean? I don't even like pastries.

DAN. – in fancy little cafés and then you proceed to tell me how little time you want to spend on it –

ANNE. That's not the impression I wanted to give you at all.

DAN. – and you think that by offering a handful of shekels to someone, you can get all the information you need, so that you can then earn a good salary and get off the island before you, heaven forbid, turn native and learn two words of the indigenous.

ANNE. That's not what I'm trying to do at all. I've been learning Gaelic.

DAN. This is so tiring.

ANNE. I'd have thought you'd have been more than happy to record these things for posterity.

DAN. People either use them, or they don't. People make up new ones, or they forget old ones.

ANNE. I've come an awful long way just to talk to you.

DAN. That is not my fault.

ANNE. Why are you being so unreasonable / about this?

DAN. Unreasonable? What do you mean, unreasonable?

ANNE. What I meant was –

DAN. Who are you to call me unreasonable? Coming to my room and calling me names. Get out of here.

ANNE. I apologise. We just got off on the wrong foot.

DAN. Get out of here.

ANNE. Fine. Fine. It's not worth the bloody hassle. Jesus Christ.

ANNE *leaves.* LUBE *comes in.*

LUBE. Foo's yer doos now, eh! Foo's yer doos now!

DAN. What?

LUBE. The quine is vanquished. My brave Cuchulainn! He grapples with his enemies at the ford and one by one their blood colours the water! Bravo! Ferdia laughs with delight!

DAN. I'm a bit tired.

LUBE. Not to worry. Not to worry. Have a seat. I am on top of the situation. Cup of tea?

DAN. No. Maybe just a rest.

DAN *lies down.*

LUBE. No problem. A rest. Let me take care of it.

DAN. It's so tiring talking to people from outside. Everything so fast.

LUBE. I know it. I was once one of the gerbils stoking that engine, so I know it well. Better off, Dan. She'd just have tired you out.

They settle down.

You forget things in here. Dan. You forget what it's like out.

Pause.

Do you remember much? Of before this?

DAN. Yes.

LUBE. You know what I remember. I remember being naked in a tin bath in front of the fire surrounded by warm water and the towels so hot and crisp on a dark wood rail. My mother. I remember the noise of Glasgow outside. That's the first thing I remember pretty much. Forget about her, Dan.

Pause.

DAN. The first thing I remember is being at the front gate of the house and the grass felt so tall on a hot hot day. I'd never felt heat like that before, probably. The sun was like a golden plum in the sky and the smoke from the chimneys went straight up and I remember looking down at my legs and being surrounded by buttercup-yellow, neoinean-white and sea-pink. Hot hot. I remember my grandfather. He used to build boats. I would go to his boat shed and there'd be a massive skeleton of a boat lying there, half-naked. And the smell of fresh wood and the steam from the machine that bends it gently. And the plans for the boat and lines of numbers written in vertical columns. His measurements for these pieces of wood. Bits of writing everywhere. Helped him remember where he was.

Pause.

LUBE. We'll be alright the two of us, eh? We'll be just fine.

DAN. Fine.

ACT TWO

DAN's *bedroom. DAN is writing and drawing intently.* ANNE *knocks at the door.*

DAN. It's you again.

ANNE. Hi.

Pause.

I wanted to say I'm sorry. For the last time. I didn't mean any offence.

DAN. That's fine.

Pause.

Well. Safe trip home.

ANNE. I was hoping just for even five minutes of your time. After I saw you I went home and talked to everyone I knew again. I made a little headway but . . . it appears that everyone else who really knows about this subject is dead. You're my last hope.

DAN. That makes me feel just splendid.

Pause.

ANNE. And I've got five hours before the next ferry . . . well, let me show you . . .

She takes out a chart.

I'm doing the whole area of your village. Robhanis. The moor, the machair. The township. There's lots of blanks but I'm still working on it.

DAN. That's my house. Just there.

ANNE. Yes.

DAN. You've not got many names written down.

ANNE. I thought, well . . . I talked to a couple of people and they told me what they knew. I've spent months walking around. Measuring. Surveying. Talking.

DAN. Walking around the village?

ANNE. All sorts of weather. Quite proud of myself, actually.

DAN. Tell me. Tell me where you walk to.

ANNE. Well, I walk about. I . . . sometimes start at the beach. Then walk up past the church. The shop. Then I take a right and walk in the road, down to the machair.

DAN. None of these places have names, do they? What road?

ANNE. The road after the church. The one that goes to the machair.

DAN. There's three roads. I wouldn't like to follow one of your maps, I wouldn't make it past the garden gate.

ANNE. My house doesn't have a garden. Well, I make my way out of my non-garden gate, to the beach, up the main road, past the church and into . . . there's a small village . . .

DAN. Baile Glaom it's called.

ANNE. Yes.

DAN. Many a day I walked up that road. I once had to walk up the road and take a bull from one end of the village to the next. It was . . . Well . . . what I meant to say. Well . . . the bull knew where it was going.

ANNE. Did it now. And where was it going?

DAN. Well, it had a meeting arranged with some cows.

ANNE. Right.

DAN. It was already . . . for the whole walk through the village. And all the girls would come out and take the mickey out of me. It was the biggest . . . longest walk of my life. I couldn't wait to get rid of that bloody bull and its . . . can I see your map?

DAN *looks at the map.*

What do you do exactly? When you make these little maps?

ANNE. When surveying an area? Well, we set up our GPS receiver for about four hours. Or even longer, that gives us a good fix. And, it's all digital now of course, but the satellites give you a fantastic accuracy. We then download the data, all the points we've recorded into our system and it gives us our basic template. Then we add the relevant data. We get data from different bodies, then compile it. But this is pretty basic stuff. You wouldn't believe the things that are possible now, even for an average person with a computer, you can download a NASA site where you can zoom into any part of the world you want, to a scale where you can see actual people. You can see seagulls sitting on top of the Washington Monument, and the images are updated every few hours. So you can imagine if any old person can get their hands on this, well, what it's like at the cutting edge. Imagine what the military can see. I'd love to work with the army. Their satellite systems. The military is the place to be when it comes to all of this. It's a great field to be in . . . so many places are still virgin territory . . . the sea-floor . . . Mars.

DAN. You walk up to the cliffs?

ANNE. Yes.

DAN. You can't show cliffs on a map.

ANNE. Yes, you can.

DAN. An island looks different from the sea. You look at it like a bird.

ANNE. Well, this particular map shows . . .

DAN. With your map you could easily ram your boat into one of them. You'd feel your wellington boots fill up and you'd find yourself slipping under the water. It's a lot of dangerous ground you're missing.

ANNE. We're not missing it.

DAN. Look, up here. Near this sgeir . . . skerry. It's called the Dolphin, in Gaelic. Because it looks like a dolphin's back, you see. An leumadair. People jump from the cliff above it. It's an irony that the literal translation of dolphin is 'the jumper'. If these people knew that, they maybe wouldn't jump. Because it makes it a little . . . humorous.You don't think it would make you feel bad?

ANNE. What?

DAN. Imagine. You work for the army. Your job is to map an area to find enemy bases. Insurgents or whatever name they call them now. You find a base. You use your mapping technology and your degree from a good university to find out everything you can about them and then the SAS are sent in to mop up. They kill fifteen people.

ANNE. That's not my responsibility. I'm just doing my job.

DAN. You don't think it's your fault? They killed three civilians. It was your work that sent them there. How does that make you feel?

ANNE. I'm not responsible for it.

DAN. You didn't pull the trigger.

ANNE. No.

DAN. Sometimes we pull the trigger without knowing it.

ANNE. So, how about this area up here, at the moment there's hardly any data on it.

DAN *puts the map down.*

DAN. You know what I think? From looking at what you've done here.

ANNE. What?

DAN. I think you don't understand.

ANNE. I can assure you I know my job inside out. Fair enough the Gaelic is sometimes hard. I'm sure it's a different shape of palate needed . . . but I've learnt enough Gaelic to make them out. Sometimes the different layers of language make it difficult. Old Norse, Gaelic, Anglicisations . . . it's a little bit like an orthographic slasher flick, but –

DAN. You don't understand them.

ANNE. Why do you say that?

DAN. You just want a list of names to fill up your map. You're not interested in who uses them. Where they come from. Why they're called what they are. You just want names. It's just your job. The sooner you do it, the sooner you can drink cappuccinos and wear high heels.

ANNE. That's a little unfair.

DAN. But there's no point unless you know what's behind them. The stories behind them. What people use the land for. How they guide you. How they anchor you.

ANNE. I don't have room for stories.

DAN. I don't think I can help you. You have no room for cliffs. You have no room for stories. What kind of map exactly are you making? One for people who don't need to find somewhere.

ANNE. I can assure you that when it comes to mapping, I know my stuff. I have a PhD from –

DAN. I have little need for an apprentice.

ANNE. I have no need of a teacher.

DAN. I think you do. (*Pause.*) You're wasting your time. I can't remember any of these places. And in the end that'll make you more angrier, you'll go home and think, that fellow made me think he was going to help me and in the end he didn't. And it'll reflect badly on me. I'm not as young as I was with the memory and everything.

ANNE. I had some photographs to show you. But I left them at the hotel.

DAN. Photographs? What kind of photographs?

ANNE. I've got photos of Robhanis. Donald showed me around the place.

DAN. Donald? Who is Donald?

ANNE. Your nephew. Donald.

Pause.

DAN. You know Donald?

ANNE. Yes. He's been helping me. I don't know what I'd do without him up there.

DAN. Photographs?

ANNE. It's a great place for taking photos. The light is / great.

DAN. Of Donald?

ANNE. Yes.

Pause.

DAN. That was a long time ago.

ANNE. I talked to his mother. She said you were an artist.

DAN. I'm not. She talked about me?

ANNE. Yes. Have I done something wrong?

DAN. No.

Pause.

I'm free tomorrow.

ANNE. So am I.

DAN. Very good. Very good.

ANNE *goes.* LUBE *comes in. He has been watching them.*

LUBE. Whew! Anybody else around here got a bit of a hard cock? She's momentous! I didn't realise the first time, but . . . whew!

DAN. You were listening to me?

LUBE. Young as well. A fresh young body beside you is worth its weight in cloves. Busy bee, you, Dan boy.

DAN. I am. Busy. And don't talk about a woman like that. What are you doing here? Eavesdropping like a seagull.

LUBE. It's a free country, isn't it? Well, apart from this hornet's nest of devils and popinjays. Anyway, she's interfering with our plans. The first time fair enough but . . . is she going to become a fixture? Like a sofa? This isn't a hospital. She can't just visit willy-nilly, grapes and *Woman's Own* and 'How are you?' and 'Auntie was asking for you' although we both know that Auntie couldn't give two bat hoots even if you were strung up by your ankles by the Spanish Imposition. No. We have to close ranks. The barbarians must stay at the gate. Barbarium pilum erectum est. Then a-fucking-gain, I will admit to the upside. It's not often we get so close to a real, breathing woman these days. Just the smell is enough. Cinnamon. The nurses in here smell of leatherback turtles.

DAN. She's going to visit me again.

LUBE. It's unavoidable?

DAN. Yes.

LUBE. Well. We could turn this to our advantageous.

DAN. How?

LUBE. We need money. And she's probably got a wallet-full. And some fancy cards. So maybe this visit might be God's way of giving us a helping hand.

DAN. I'm not going to steal from her.

LUBE. Don't look at it as stealing, look at it as taking what's rightfully yours. The nation owes you a debt, Dan. It's terrible, old soldiers selling matchboxes on street corners.

Pause.

DAN. I'm not going to do it, Lube.

LUBE. If our plan fails, it'll be because of you.

DAN. We don't have any plans.

LUBE. That's good, Dan. Throws people off the scent. You're right. (*Winks.*) We don't have any plans. I brought a present for you. A present. Very Buddhist that, they're always living in the present. No? Not want it?

DAN. What is it?

LUBE. This'll cast all despondency to the four winds.

LUBE *brings out a bottle of beer.*

Look what I have. Lovely lovely. A beer. I sneaked it in. It certainly makes the saliva run down the moo. Sneaky sneaky cheeky cheeky. Come on. Let's have it. Opener. Aha!

He tries to get the top off with his teeth. DAN *eventually takes it off him and twists the screwtop off. They share a drink. Furtively.*

Oooh. Good.

DAN. Good good.

LUBE. Good excellent.

DAN. Excellent good.

Pause.

I want to speak to her by myself. Next time she comes.

LUBE. Why? You wouldn't want to deprive me of images for my night-time pastime?

DAN. That's disgusting.

LUBE. It's natural, my little Presbyterian eunuch.

DAN. You don't treat women proper.

LUBE. Do I sense a little loving interest myself?

DAN. No.

LUBE. Long-ago feelings bubbling to the surface again?

DAN. No. I've told you not to talk about these things.

LUBE. You're as closed as a pebble sometimes.

DAN. I don't feel like that about her.

LUBE. Methink the lady doth protesteth too much.

Pause.

You know, I don't miss too much in this piss-hole-in-the-snow type of place. But I miss a cool beer with the sweating beads on the outside running down the pane of glass and a cool head on it like freshly milked cream. Imagine this. Coming home after a hard day's work. She's been working on her maps and it's made her a bit sweaty –

DAN. Stop that.

LUBE. She kisses you as you come in the door. Your dog runs up to you. She's busy taking your tea out of the oven. It's macaroni cheese. Your favourite. She leans over to kiss you.

DAN. You're going to kill us both if you carry on saying things like that.

Pause. They drink.

LUBE. I had a sweetheart once. It didn't finish well. But she was very sweet to me. We had a beautiful little girl together. I miss that little girl. Do you have children?

DAN. No.

LUBE. Well, you wouldn't understand. There's no missing like it. I feel like someone is squeezing my heart, from the moment I wake up in the morning to when I finally escape to sleep. I have the image of her fleeting in front of my thoughts every moment. But I know she's probably changed now. They grow so quickly. And when I think of what her mother is saying to her. Even God-like Achilles has no chance.

Pause.

Two beers bad. Four beers good.

DAN. Pill beer bad.

LUBE. Pill beer good! A toast to Seonaidh! The beer-drinking sea god! Seonaidh, if you were here I would gladly pour this harvest gift into your salty sea-water innards. If we hadn't deserted you, we wouldn't be in this mess what we are. Why do you think we're in here? Because we forgot to give him thanks. We got too busy buying toasters and worrying about dog insurance. Catalogues and clothes and cookers and cats and women. When do we get to actually live our lives-

DAN. I live my life.

LUBE. No you don't. You're in here, wall-bouncing. Too scared! Too scared to step outside.

DAN. I just need a rest.

LUBE. Oh, give it a break. You and your rest. How many years . . . fifteen . . . ! Fucking Lazarus –

DAN. Fourteen.

LUBE. – would be embarrassed by you.

DAN. Fourteen. Fourteen.

LUBE. Come on, Dan. You're tormenting me with this volunteer fucking nonsense! This isn't where you're supposed to be! Tormenting my very inside of head until it explodes and ghosts.

DAN. I've been thinking about your plan. I think I'll leave it.

LUBE. Leave it. You'll leave it? After all our hard work.

DAN. We haven't done any work.

LUBE. Thinking is work. Thinking is bloody hard work, these days.

DAN. We have endless amounts of time to think. We're practically made of time.

LUBE. Dan! For fucks-fucks-fuck's sake! Why do you think I'm off the pills! Training! That's why. Training for when we leave this place. You're acting as if something bad is going to happen if you do something . . . wrong, but what could be WORSE THAN THIS PLACE! WHAT COULD BE FUCKING WORSE THAN THIS FUCKING PLACE! We're hidden away from the world. This is the worst thing any man can imagine! And you're happy to be here. Not only that, you asked to be here! There's nothing stopping you from walking out the door! What's wrong with you?

DAN. I have my reasons to be here. I don't need to share them with you or anybody else.

LUBE. What's so wrong with you that you wouldn't just love to walk down a street with the sun breaking on the railings and the green and gold of the trees? And to laugh without it echoing off the walls. And to sit by yourself in a pub reading a newspaper?

DAN. I . . . have had . . . enough.

LUBE. How do you what do you mean, enough?

DAN. Since the moment I met you – no, let me rephrase that – ever since you foisted yourself through the door, you've done nothing but ask me questions and bounce around in here and talked and talked and talked and questions and questions what about this what about that and let me tell you about any sort of nonsense I choose and how about this when I was young isn't this a fascinating story and welcome to the circus. When I was perfectly happy not thinking of these things. I don't want to think. I don't want to think. And then you proceed to advise me, like some half-arsed bank manager, what I should be doing. And frankly, what business is it of yours? You don't know me –

LUBE. I know you better than you think.

DAN. – from Methuselah and just because I was unfortunate enough to leave my door open an iota –

LUBE. Iota is a good word.

DAN. – some cosmic powers of some kind have decided to inflict some divine retribution on me for some reason or other.

LUBE. Karma.

DAN. I want to enjoy my day without some amadan / disturbing me.

LUBE. Amadan? Who are you calling amadan? Idiot, is it now? Now it's idiot, is it? As easy as kiss my hand, out he comes with it.

LUBE pushes DAN.

DAN. If ever there was a bigger amadan to walk God's earth, he's yet to reveal himself.

DAN pushes LUBE back. They tussle as they talk.

Well, it's the end of this particular hyena party, and . . . yes . . . and yes . . . you come in. You move things about. You move things about as if you own them! Stones! Chairs! You make a mockery of this room. As if the world was one big room belonging to you!

LUBE. Your life was one long well of boredom before you met me.

DAN. Well, I've had enough of it! I want boredom! I want peace and quiet again! I don't want to plan bad escapes! I don't want to build aeroplanes! I want to walk in the gardens and then come back here for a cup of tea and a small biscuit.

LUBE. Who the fuck mentioned aeroplanes?

They stop fighting.

DAN. You did.

LUBE. Don't be so stupid. Where would you hide an aeroplane in here?

Pause. They sit down. They share a beer.

ACT THREE

DAN*'s room. The next day. A knock at the door. It is* ANNE.

ANNE. Is it alright to visit?

DAN. The map woman. I thought it might be Lube.

ANNE. Lube?

DAN. My friend.

Pause.

ANNE. I've got the photos we talked about. And something else.

ANNE *takes out a laptop.*

I thought you might like to see the place in glorious Technicolor.
I've got a little film for you. I've got photos as well, but I
thought I would show you this first. This is just a little project
for me. I don't quite understand yet what I'm trying to do. Even.
But I thought maybe if I looked at the places in a way that I
could . . . edit them. I went up to . . . Toll . . . how do you say it?

DAN. Toll a' Ròidh.

ANNE. Yes. Well . . . Donald took me up there to film.

DAN. This film of yours isn't . . .

ANNE. Isn't what?

DAN. You don't have . . . people in a small boat. Pretending to be
Vikings. Because if that's the type of film it is, I don't want to
see it.

ANNE. Give me some credit, eh.

She plays the film on the computer. DAN *gradually moves closer
to it.*

DAN. My word. Isn't that amazing. You made that yourself? Look
at that. That's the Sùil, there. Those cliffs. The graveyard. Toll a'
Ròidh . . . who is that fellow?

ANNE. Donald.

DAN. Really? Donald? But he's a man.

32

ANNE. He is.

Pause.

DAN. That's quite something, isn't it? What a place. Isn't it . . .
have you been down to the arch? Toll a' Ròidh? Have you?

ANNE. Not down to it.

DAN. Why not?

ANNE. Donald didn't have time that day.

DAN. You didn't go down by yourself?

ANNE. No.

DAN. I suppose it's better to be shown the way by someone. How
about Dun Eistean? Luchraban?

ANNE. That looks a little bit dangerous.

DAN. You'll never make a map of the place if you don't feel the
earth under your toes. The climb to Luchraban is a good one.
You pick your moment. You go when the tide has gone out
enough to cross. Not when the tide is coming in. It's a little
steep right enough, but you're up and over the top before you
know it. Then you get to see the place properly. Buried in the
ground, three cells. Peregrine-built.

LUBE *comes in.*

LUBE. Another day another dollar, holy man. What's this?

DAN. Just a video Anne made.

ANNE *stops the video.*

ANNE. Hello.

LUBE. You have visitor, Dan?

ANNE. Excuse me, we're a little busy at the moment.

LUBE. Busy shmusy. You must be Dan's charming friend, Anne.
Foos yer doos, as they say in French.

ANNE. You must be Lube. Pleased to meet you. As I said, Dan and
I are quite busy at the moment. I'll be leaving fairly soon if you
want to –

DAN. It's OK, Anne.

ANNE *busies herself with her laptop.*

LUBE. Yes. Lube is just passing. You're looking a bit peely-wally, Dan. Is the end nigh, my little Calvinist friend? The thought of sin flattening you to the ground like a tractor tyre.

DAN. I'm fine.

LUBE. How was the doctor? You had an appointment in the morning, first thing, yes? Am I not correct?

DAN. Yes.

LUBE. Well?

DAN. Fine.

LUBE. Fine? Fine, you say?

DAN. I'm fine.

LUBE. I've got an appointment with the doctor. Myself. Imminently.

DAN. Do you?

LUBE. Any idea what it's about?

DAN. No.

LUBE. You'd better not have given me some kind of bloody lurgy. We need to be in the top of health. I forgive you, of course. But we must be careful of people coming in, willy-nilly. We are like the naked people of the New World and she is like dirty, dirty Columbus with his rats and Spaniards and tuberculosis and sausages.

ANNE. Would that be the cat's mother you're talking about?

LUBE (*to* DAN). Not offering me a seat?

DAN. Have a seat.

LUBE. No thanks. I know my place.

DAN. Don't be daft.

LUBE. Anyway, I'd rather be in a room with Mexicans prodding my goolies with cattle poles than be around this sickening love-in for a moment longer. Oh yes, it's obvious.

ANNE. What's obvious?

LUBE. Coo . . . coo. Little love doves.

ANNE. I'm sorry?

34

LUBE. He hasn't been able to stop talking about you since you arrived. He's even thinking of painting a picture of you.

DAN. That's not true.

LUBE. Deny it not, knave. For I seest thine horniness through thine trews. And hearest it through the walls of thine wanking bower.

DAN. Stop it. If you'd been in the army, you'd have been taught a lesson a long time ago.

LUBE. Why? What would you have done?

DAN. Taught you a lesson. People like you need a lesson taught them.

LUBE. People like me? What does that mean, people like me?

DAN. Exactly what it says.

LUBE. Well, you're not in the fucking army any more.

DAN. I want you to stop speaking to me like this.

LUBE. Piss off.

DAN. I want you to stop speaking to me like this.

LUBE. Remember our deal.

ANNE. Shall I call for a doctor?

LUBE. Trying to get rid of me? Oh yes, with me out of the way, you can get Dan to do all of your work for you. You think a little flash of your admittedly pert breasts is going to make us go all soft for you. Well, I'll talk to the warden if you carry on being so aggressive. I know your type, is this the kind of woman you get outside now, is it?

DAN. Lube. Stop it.

LUBE. Et tu, Dan?

DAN. I think it's best if you leave.

LUBE (*to* DAN). See now? Do you understand now?

  LUBE *leaves.*

DAN. Sorry about that.

ANNE. Is your friend always in such good form?

DAN. Likes to give it. Can't take it. And anyway, what he was saying wasn't true. I wonder if the doctor told him the same thing as he told me. He's not going to be happy. He's not going to be happy at all. He might be happy. I don't know. The doctor was telling me they're going to close this place.

ANNE. And Lube doesn't know that yet?

DAN. They tell us one at a time. They tell us the place is closing. And that they think that this would be a good thing for you to do. For me to do. For one to do. That's why they're meeting us all one by one. Like Noah.

Pause.

ANNE. And what do they think you should do?

DAN. They said that I should go home to home. To Robhanis. And a nurse would check up on me in my own place. My own house. I had decided not to, but . . . I could almost see myself stepping on the ferry. Seeing the water go by. Seeing the long arms of the bay.

ANNE. And what do you think of that?

DAN. I think just a little more time here would be good. And it's . . . I don't know what people would think.

Pause.

They're planning to turn this into a hotel.

ANNE. I maybe won't be rushing to book a weekend break here.

Pause.

You have a lot to share with people. If you'd only share it.

DAN. I don't think I do. Have a lot to share.

ANNE. You do.

Pause.

DAN. This is strange work for a woman. Maps. What does your husband think of it?

ANNE. I'm not married. Well, except to my work.

DAN. You won't meet anyone wandering around cliffs and machair.

ANNE. I suppose sometimes I wonder if I'm working too hard. But you have to if you want to get ahead. Especially when it's quite a male profession. And that stuff about women not being able to read maps doesn't help. Then you get into the stream and it's

hard to come out of it. And being sent to the outer reaches . . .
somewhere remote, in a work sense, doesn't help. Promotions.
So you spend all your time being good, better, than men. And
the time gently slips away.

Pause.

DAN. You remind me a little of her. Just there.

ANNE. Who?

DAN. The way you tilted your head there. Isn't it strange the
echoes we see in people of others? Or maybe we imagine them.

Pause.

I haven't told you the truth. Sometimes.

ANNE. No?

DAN. Donald isn't my nephew.

ANNE. What do you mean?

DAN. He's my son.

Pause.

So you see, how can I go home? You see the kind of person I
am?

ANNE. Your son?

DAN. My fiancée. Her name was Mary. We were very young, but
we wanted to have the child. We married quickly and everything
was . . . Everything was wonderful. I did love her so. I was
getting on well in the army. And then she died when she had the
baby. In childbirth she died.

ANNE. I'm so sorry.

DAN. I was different then. I was hard to the world. I loved my
wife, of course. And it was the most terrible thing when I lost
her. But I was so strong. You see. In the body. I didn't think it
would enter me so badly. And it was just going to be impossible.
What did I know about a young child? A baby. My sister had
tried and tried to have a child but she couldn't. And so it was
decided that she would raise it as her own.

ANNE. Didn't people know?

DAN. She lived in Glasgow at the time. Then I was posted to
Ireland. And I tried to forget about it all. Ireland was a good place

to forget things at that time. But I couldn't. I couldn't. The things we did there. It made me lose myself even more. My family. What kind of man gives away his child? What kind of man?

ANNE. I still think you're a good person.

DAN. Why are you saying these things?

ANNE. I want to see you in a better place.

DAN. I'm in the place I deserve.

ANNE. Why do you say that? These things you've told me about, you can get through it. You can tell Donald the truth.

DAN. Please don't tell Donald.

ANNE. Of course I won't. It doesn't mean you can't go home.

Pause.

DAN. I think you're good at it. Your work.

ANNE. Do you?

LUBE *comes in.*

LUBE. Horse manure! Come on, Dan. There's not a moment to be lost. Set the topgallants. Let go the main.

DAN. What's wrong?

LUBE. Have they told you?

DAN. Told me what?

LUBE. Have they told you what? They must have told you what.

DAN. Told me what?

LUBE. That the place is going to close.

DAN. Yes.

LUBE. Yes?

DAN. Yes.

LUBE. You didn't tell me?

DAN. No.

LUBE. Well, we'll let it pass. There's not a moment to be lost. I've got everything prepared. You'll excuse me . . . Miss . . . what the hell is your name anyway? Anyway, time to go for you. The adults have things they need to be doing.

ANNE. Maybe Dan has other plans.

LUBE. I'm sure Dan can talk for himself, Miss Lady. Honestly, I came into this room simply wanting to rectify a situation but you just won't let it rest. You threaten me. You demean me. And now you order my friend around like a pomeranian dog –

DAN. I'm not going to the same place as you.

LUBE. Don't be so daft.

DAN. I'm not. They've asked me if I want to go home.

LUBE. Home?

DAN. To the island.

LUBE. And what did you say?

DAN. I said I didn't know.

LUBE. Implying that you might?

DAN. I haven't decided.

LUBE. They didn't give you a choice to go where I was going? The choice to come with me?

DAN. No.

LUBE. You're going to leave me?

DAN. I've no choice.

LUBE. But whatever you decide, you're going to leave me.

Pause.

ANNE. Don't worry, Dan.

LUBE *goes over to a box of* DAN's *maps, picks them up and throws them across the room.*

Stop that.

LUBE. Get tae. Come on, Dan. Don't do this to us.

DAN. No.

LUBE. She's turned you against me. Hasn't she?

DAN. It's nothing to do with her.

LUBE. I've been a best friend to you and you repay me like this, sloping off at the first sniff.

ANNE. If you don't leave, I'll call security.

LUBE. I thought I told you to get tae, you don't even live here. Come with me, Dan. Now's the time. Let's go. Together.

ANNE. I don't think that's wise, Dan.

LUBE. What do you know! You bloody witch! Interloper! What do you know! She's trying to steal it, Dan. All the names she's collecting from you. I've been keeping an eye on her, Dan. She's going to publish it all under her own name.

ANNE. That's not true.

LUBE *picks up a map and rips it.*

LUBE. Eh? I'll do that to all of them. That'll pay you out.

DAN. Leave them alone.

LUBE *rips another one.*

Don't do that!

LUBE. Does Achilles bow down to threats? I'll tear the keel from under your boat and make sure that this is one Helen you won't set sail with.

ANNE *tries to leave.* LUBE *gets in her way.*

ANNE. Get out of my way.

LUBE. You're not going anywhere.

DAN. Stop this!

DAN *pushes* LUBE *out of the way and positions himself between* LUBE *and* ANNE. LUBE *picks himself up.*

Anne, I think you should call the doctor.

LUBE. The doctor?

DAN. Go on, Anne.

ANNE. I don't think I should leave you alone with him.

DAN. I can take care of myself.

LUBE. Halle-fucking-lujah!

DAN. Calm down.

LUBE. Piss off.

DAN. Lube. Calm down.

LUBE. What are you, a parrot? Gog-gag!

DAN. Calm down.

LUBE. Coming over the hard man, now. The squaddie.

DAN. I want you to leave.

LUBE. Come on, Dan. Everything'll be fine once she goes. Surely you can see that.

DAN. Lube, I want you to leave. Just go.

LUBE. So this is how you repay me? You had nothing before you met me. Nothing in here. No other friends to speak of. And you've broken my heart, Dan. I thought we had found a way to get through it. But you couldn't let it be, there. I rue the day that ever I called you friend. Judas. Three cockerels!

DAN. Anne's going to get a doctor, Lube. They'll look after you.

LUBE. You bastards. Judas bastards. Calling hunters after me. I connay you. I connay what you're doing. She's made you lose yourself. You think my gomballs can't see what's coming. Selling me up to white-coated butchers wanting meat for their block. Rajes. Bloody rajes!

DAN. Lube. You're ill. You're not taking your medicine.

LUBE. Stay away from me! Tie me like a sheep, ropes on flank and burning pain and brightbulb off in my tete, smoke belching out my neb! This is what you want? You want no bright gumball float thoughts left for Lube? You want them to stick me up? You want them to tie me up?

DAN. You need some help, Lube. You're upset.

LUBE. Hurt-bearers like a swarm of wasps gold-banding me. You think so little of me. You think so little as this of me.

DAN. I'm trying to help you.

LUBE. I'll fucking kill you!

DAN *goes up to him. He looks like a soldier.*

DAN. Don't fucking push it. Now get out of here or I'll give you a thrashing you'll remember on your deathbed.

LUBE *leaves. Everything is topsy-turvy in the room.* ANNE *goes out. She comes back a few moments later.*

ANNE. I spoke to one of the doctors just outside. They'll take care of him.

ANNE *tries to help him put things together again.*

Are you OK, Dan?

DAN. Just leave it.

ANNE. Shall I get you a doctor as well?

DAN. No.

He picks up the ripped maps.

Everything I touch, it breaks.

ANNE. That's not true.

DAN. Everything. I'm trained to. To break things. To break people. They train you. To kill people. They make you shoot targets which look like people so you don't stop yourself when you see a real person. They train you to forget all of that. And then when they're done with you, they throw you out on the street. They don't think to ask what all that killing does to you. They make you lose yourself.

I just needed a rest after the war. The desert. I needed a rest after the desert. I drank a lot, it helped. I just wanted peace and quiet. It would come back to me without asking. I would walk when I came back, down Piccadilly and I would see burnt bodies on the pavements. I just wanted a rest from it. But I wasn't supposed to be here so long.

Pause.

I didn't mean to do it, you know. I prayed and prayed afterwards.

ANNE. Didn't mean to do what?

DAN. It was an order. We were clearing from house to house. A wee town somewhere. God, it was so hot, you could almost feel the soles of your shoes melting. I can see it exactly, even now. That's just what I was told to do. It's what I was told to do. If you go into a room and it's suspect. You fire into it. If there are . . . people. People you don't know if they're alive or dead. Friend or foe lying on the ground. You shoot into them before you turn them over. Otherwise, you never know, they might turn round and stick a knife in your gut. Be hiding a revolver. And so that's what I did. But I turned the body around and it was a woman. She was holding her child. These rounds are powerful, they destroy. It had gone through them both. A whole family. Because of me. Another family.

DAN *breaks down a bit.*

God have mercy on me. God have mercy on me. I deserve my place in hell for what I've done.

ANNE. It wasn't your fault. Dan, it wasn't your fault.

DAN. It was.

ANNE. You were a soldier.

DAN. A soldier doesn't do that. He does right. It's my own fault. See. Come here.

DAN *takes out some maps. They are of the village in Iraq where the incident took place.*

That's the way we went in. Here's the house here. See. That's the house. That's it. That's the . . .

Pause.

It'll be over quicker this way.

ANNE. What will?

DAN. My life.

ANNE. Please don't say that, Dan.

ANNE *looks at one or two of the drawings dotted about.* ANNE *lifts one of the maps* DAN *has drawn.*

DAN. The doctors are going to take care of Lube?

ANNE. They said they would.

DAN. Good.

Pause.

I can't talk about your maps today.

ANNE. That's fine. I didn't bring my things, anyway.

DAN. Your things?

ANNE. My charts and stuff. Pens and stuff. I brought the photos and the film for you but that's all. I just . . . wanted to see you.

DAN. What do you mean?

ANNE. I just wanted to see you.

DAN. You came because you . . . you wanted to see me?

ANNE. Yes.

Pause.

DAN. If you stand here. Come on. Stand here. You look out in this direction and you see the various points in front of you. Headlands. Cliffs. We can start from here. Walk from here. You are standing on a small cliff. It's a small cliff which is just the right height to fish from using a bamboo rod. My neighbour's grandmother, Peigi Iain Bhain, used to go fishing there, she'd put the potatoes on and by the time they were almost done she would be back with a pail of fish, lovely fish. So that's where she would go. Sgeir a' Leadaidh. The Lady's Skerry.

ANNE. That's a good story.

DAN. Whether it's good or not. That's undecided. But that's why it's called that. You walk this way. You pass Sgeir an Crubag. That's where they went for crabs.

Next there is a spring which comes up from the ground. A clean clean spring with beautiful clear water. And there was a girl in the village who became very ill when she was young . . . maybe it was a pregnancy, she was very young though. Her mother tried everything but nothing worked until as a last chance she took her daughter to the spring and people had always said that the spring helped cure sickness and some people that was the reason they drank a little from it fairly often or if they passed by they would always give the spring their attention and that's what she did, washed her daughter nearly naked in the spring, close to death she was, you could see the greyness in her face and the breath rattling in her stomach. And it was then that on the water touching her forehead the clank of her breath became gentler and some buttercup colour came back to her face. And that woman who was on the starsach, star-looking last journey with the last breath about to be given and taken from her, she lived till she was an old old woman and she knew many people who left us before she did. And her name was Mairi. And every time she went past the fuaran cold fuar water, she took a sip of it to remind her. And it was then that people started to call it Tobar Mhàiri. Mary's Well.

And so you see. I've hardly taken a step and your map is full already.

ANNE. How do you remember all of it?

DAN. It's easy. And I write it down. Look.

DAN *goes to the linen cupboard and takes out a bedsheet. He lets it fly, it is covered with details of a map. He shows another one to her. Some of his designs are geometric shapes. Some are mind-maps of villages. Some are lists of place names. There are representations of some of the places he has told* ANNE *about. She holds one or two of them up.*

ANNE. The stones. That's why you always have stones about, isn't it? To weigh them down.

DAN. They fly away easy. See, I write them down in little as well.

He shows her some notebooks. She picks up some of the bedsheets.

ANNE. What is this one?

DAN. Ronan. Saint Ronan. When he travelled on the back of the sea monster.

ANNE. And this one?

DAN. That's . . . Toll a' Ròidh. Where the Vikings tried to pull the island back to Scandinavia.

ANNE. And this one?

DAN. That's Tobar Mhàiri. Mary's Well where the woman was cured by the water.

ANNE. They're beautiful. You're an artist.

DAN. I don't think I am.

ANNE. The land remembers. Marks from all these people that have gone before. It makes my maps look a little dry, doesn't it?

DAN. Maybe a little bit . . . bare. But that's nothing that can't be fixed. With a bit of time.

Pause.

ANNE. Do you have much more?

DAN. A bit.

DAN *brings out his book of maps. He spreads maps out on the floor. He opens more drawers and they are full of his work, soon the floor of the room is covered. The massive sheets are unfolded.* DAN *eventually sits and looks at it all.*

ANNE. Just one or two things, then.

DAN. Yes.

ANNE. You must spend all your time doing this.

DAN. Yes.

DAN *digs around the maps.*

There's another story. At Traigh Shanndaidh, when the weather caught some boats coming back from the fishing and –

ANNE. Stop.

DAN. What stop, what do you mean, stop?

ANNE. Dan, this is all amazing . . . but . . . it's just . . . (*Pause.*) What are you doing here?

DAN. I'm showing you maps. Some maps.

ANNE. No. What are you doing here? In this place? If you spend all your time thinking of another place?

Pause.

DAN. I needed a rest.

ANNE. Don't you think it's time, Dan? What are you doing here?

DAN. I don't know any more.

ANNE. What do you want, Dan?

DAN. I don't know any more. I just need some peace and quiet.

ANNE. I don't believe you.

DAN. I just need a little more time.

ANNE. No, you don't.

DAN. Not long. That's not what I mean.

ANNE. This place is closing, Dan. What do you want?

Pause.

DAN. I would have five minutes sitting at the cliffs sloping gently down into the cold sea, sea-pink cliffs and the sky as blue as an eye. And hear the sounds of the birds wheeling and floating nearby with the cool breeze from the north on my face.

That blast of colour and wind breath and shafting light and wind-fed horizon cloud. My lungs would be full of scented air, my ears with the dull touch of waves and my eyes filled with the coloured floor before me.

I would arch up and feel my cloud hands holding sky and see it lying flat in front of me. Open. Immovable. Constant, constant earth. Beautiful. I would count these places out one more time. To feel their time-edged names on my lips, how sweet that would be.

I would look out over this oval horizon with my gaze fixed on the far line, as I stand on the crumbling lip of this place. I would be part and the same as everything, the sky and part of the cliffs and the sea. That would make me happy. So happy. I would be a crow. I would be a wave. I would be a beautiful day. I would go home.

I want to go home.

He breaks down a little.

I want to go home.

I want to go home.

ANNE. Why don't you just do that, then?

ANNE starts to pick up maps. DAN gets up and they quietly start to tidy up the room together.

The light changes around them. We hear birds, the sounds of the country. Light floods the room. As the tidying finishes and the lid is closed on DAN's army trunk, we are back in Robhanis. ANNE is with him. They are standing outside.

So that's . . . Traigh Shanndaidh . . . Toll a' Ròidh. Over there . . . Luchraban . . .

DAN. That's it. Shall we climb down? It's low tide so we can get over to the island.

ANNE. Yes.

They start off. DAN waits for a moment, looking around him.

DAN. A beautiful day.

He leaves.

End.

A Nick Hern Book

I was a Beautiful Day first published in Great Britain
as a paperback original in 2005 by Nick Hern Books Limited,
14 Larden Road, London W3 7ST in association with
the Traverse Theatre, Edinburgh

Cover image: Euan Myles

Typeset by Country Setting, Kingsdown, Kent CT14 8ES
Printed in Great Britain by Cox and Wyman, Reading, Berks

A CIP catalogue record for this book is available from
the British Library

ISBN-13   978 1 85459 913 1
ISBN-10   1 85459 913 5